THE PARABLES OF JAMES E. TALMAGE

Compiled by
Albert L. Zobell, Jr.

Published By
Deseret Book Company
Salt Lake City, Utah
1973

Copyright 1973
By
Deseret Book Co.
Library of Congress Catalog Card No. 73-77367
ISBN No. 0-87747-4958

Printed In U.S.A.
by
Deseret Press

Compiler's Note

On a summery Sabbath morning the deacons quorum adviser said: "You, you, and you—make a report on the Articles of Faith next Sunday."

"But I won't be here next time," I protested.

(He knew that. My mother had passed away the summer before after a more than seven-years' illness that had been touch and go from the beginning. During the previous schoolyear our home had been held together by a succession of hired housekeepers. But life was easier and happier during the summer. My father had year-around railroad work; he was home one day in three, and when he was home it was almost like old-times for my younger sister and me, and when he was away, with no school responsibilities to claim us, we were more than welcome at relatives' homes. That also meant that we were in our own ward meetings one Sunday in three.)

"You will be here next Sunday. No excuses."

Characteristically I forgot about the assignment until almost bedtime the following Saturday. Then I discussed it with my father.

"Dr. James E. Talmage of the Council of the

Twelve knows more about the Articles of Faith than anyone else I know. There's a book of his on the shelf," he said.

I found the book, turned to the pages that would cover my assignment, and as I muttered "this is good," my father was on the telephone making arrangements with an aunt to delay coming for us until after priesthood meeting.

As I was called upon the next morning I opened the book and began to read. It was the first time that I had tried to read Dr. Talmage's explanation in his marvelous vocabulary aloud, and the attempt was disastrous.

The deacons adviser could not shield his disgust, and with less than magnificent words announced that it would have been better if I had failed to come that morning if I couldn't do better than that.

There was my invitation to cease Church attendance and activity for the rest of my life. (Looking back on it, I have understood some of my non-active friends from various parts of the Church who certainly possessed more promise than I.) Fortunately the invitation for me was withdrawn; as I returned to Sunday meetings the next time my father was home it was noted that I had had a birthday and it was proposed that I be ordained a teacher.

Over the years Dr. Talmage (a living General Authority during my Aaronic Priesthood days) and his writings and speeches became a personal challenge to me. I discovered that many of his contributions contained unforgettable stories and incidents that delightfully taught great truths in a superb way.

The Parables of James E. Talmage were found in *The Improvement Era* beginning in January 1914, but not in consecutive issues. They have been reprinted in *The Millennial Star*, "The Church News" section of *The Deseret News*, *Liahona-The Elders' Journal*, and possibly other periodicals of the Church. To me the Parables are as vital and enjoyable as the day they were written.

And now, to Helen and to John, the surviving children (in 1973), of Dr. Talmage: Many thanks for having such a wonderful teacher as a father, and I do appreciate the opportunity of placing his Parables again in print.

—Albert L. Zobell, Jr.

Table of Contents

Compiler's Note	iii
The Parable of Two Lamps	1
The Parable of the Defective Battery	7
The Parable of the Photographic Plate	13
The Parable of the Owl Express	19
The Parable of the Minted Coin	23
The Parable of the Unwise Bee	29
The Parable of the Treasure-Vault	33
The Parable of the Grateful Cat	37
The Parable of the Broken Flask	41
The Parable of the House Party and the Weather	45
The Parable of the Crystal	55
Our Lord—The Christ	59
The Life of James E. Talmage	63

The Parable of Two Lamps

Among the material things of the past—things that I treasure for sweet memory's sake and because of pleasant association in bygone days—is a lamp. It is of the Argand type, commonly known in the day of its popularity as the "Student's Lamp," so named in acknowledgment of its particular and peculiar suitability for the reader's table. Lamps of this kind were among the best in the long-ago. A very few years divide the long-ago from the present as measured in terms of improvement and progress. In the long-ago of which I speak, illuminating gas was known only in large cities or in pretentious towns with a history, and electric lights in dwellings was a rare novelty. Candles and oil lamps were the only common means of domestic illumination.

The lamp of which I speak, the student lamp of my school and college days, was one of the best of its kind. I had bought it with hard-earned savings; it was counted among my most cherished possessions. That type of lamp was provided with a small hollow wick, and had a straight cylindrical chimney, with a constriction near the base, where an enlargement adapted it to the burner. It was constructed in accordance with the best knowledge of the day. Its tubular wick, less than a fingerbreadth in diameter, with efficient air inlet at the bottom, insured fairly complete combustion with a minimum loss of energy through useless generation of heat. The oil reservoir was supported on an upright standard, removed by several inches from the place of combustion; and in consequence, the holder cast no shadow upon printed page or writing tablet, provided, of course, the lamp was properly placed.

I took good care of my lamp. I had in it a pride such as the horseman feels in his favorite mount. He likes personally to groom and feed his steed, and so I allowed none but myself to trim the wick, burnish the chimney, and fill the reservoir of my lamp. When brightly burning, with its deep green opaque shade, brilliantly deflecting and reflecting beneath, it diffused a wholly satisfactory illumination upon my page; and, as I kept vigil night after night, through the late and early hours, my lamp came to be more than a mere physical illuminator—it was a sympathetic companion, an inspiration to mental and spiritual enlightenment. You who have been in stress and strife, you who have had to wrestle with difficulty and contend with seeming fate, you who have been blessed through all such taxing strain with a never-failing friend, an ever-present and ever-ready companion—you may know somewhat of the affection I felt and feel for my faithful lamp.

Compared with waxen candle and ordinary oil burning lamps it was of high efficiency. What matters it today that such a lamp is counted dim? It was the best I knew; it was excellent in its time. Do you ask how much light it gave? I can answer your query with precision, for as early as that time, in the long-ago, I was a student of science; and I had tested my lamp according to the laws of photometry in the improvised laboratory I had contrived. The light was of about twelve candle power, in terms of the generally recognized and standardized rating. It was brilliant in that period—in the long-ago, remember.

One summer evening I sat musing studiously and withal restfully in the open air outside the door of the room in which I lodged and studied. A stranger approached. I noticed that he carried a satchel. He was affable and entertaining. I brought another chair from within, and we chatted together till the twilight had deepened into dusk, the dusk into darkness.

Then he said: "You are a student, and doubtless have much work to do o'nights. What kind of lamp do you use?" And without waiting for a reply he continued: "I have a superior lamp I should like to show you, a lamp designed and constructed according to the latest achievements of applied science, far surpassing anything heretofore produced as a means of artificial lighting."

I replied with confidence, and I confess not without some exultation: "My friend, I have a lamp, one that has been tested and proved. It has been to me a companion through many a long night. It is an Argand lamp, and one of the best. I have trimmed and cleaned it today; it is ready for the lighting. Step inside; I will show you my lamp, then you may tell me whether yours can possibly be better."

We entered my study room, and with a feeling which I assume is akin to that of the athlete about to enter a contest with one whom he regards as a pitiably inferior opponent, I put the match to my well-trimmed Argand.

My visitor was voluble in his praise. It was the best lamp of its kind he said. He averred that he had never seen a lamp in better trim. He turned the wick up and down and pronounced the adjustment perfect. He declared that never before had he realized how satisfactory a student lamp could be.

I liked the man; he seemed to me wise, and he assuredly was ingratiating. Love me, love my lamp, I thought, mentally paraphrasing a common expression of the period.

"Now," said he, "with your permission I'll light *my* lamp." He took from his satchel a lamp then known as the "Rochester." It had a chimney which, compared with mine, was as a factory smoke-stack alongside a house flue. Its hollow wick was wide enough to admit my four fingers. Its light made bright the remotest corner of my room. In its brilliant blaze my own little Argand wick burned a weak, pale yellow. Until that moment of convincing demonstration I had never known the dim obscurity in which I had lived and labored, studied and struggled.

"I'll buy your lamp," said I; "you need neither explain nor argue further." I took my new acquisition to the laboratory that same night, and determined its capacity. It turned at over forty-eight candle power—fully four times the intensity of my student lamp.

Two days after purchasing, I met the lamp-peddler on the street, about noontime. To my inquiry he replied that business was good; the demand for his lamps was greater than the factory supply. "But," said I, "you are not working today?" His rejoinder was a lesson. "Do you think that I would be so foolish as to go around trying to sell lamps in the daytime? Would you have bought one if I had lighted it for you when the sun was shining? I chose the time to show the superiority of my lamp over yours; and you were eager to own the better one I offered, were you not?"

Such is the story. Now consider the application of a part, a very small part, thereof.

"Let your light so shine before men, that they may see your good works, and glorify your Father, which is in heaven."

The man who would sell me a lamp did not disparage mine. He placed his greater light alongside my feebler flame, and I hasted to obtain the better.

The missionary servants of the Church of Jesus Christ today are sent forth, not to assail or ridicule the beliefs of men, but to set before the world a superior light, by which the smoky dimness of the flickering flames of man-made creeds shall be apparent. The work of the Church is constructive, not destructive.

As to the further meaning of the parable, let him that hath eyes and a heart see and understand.

The Parable of the Defective Battery

In the course of certain laboratory investigations I had need of a primary electric current of considerable power. My assistant prepared a voltaic battery consisting of a dozen cells of simple type. He followed the usual procedure, but, as I discovered later, gave inadequate attention to the details—those seeming trifles that make or mar perfection.

Each cell consisted of a cylindrical jar, containing an acid liquid in which were immersed a pair of plates, one of carbon, the other of zinc. The cells were connected "in series," so that the strength of the battery was the sum of the power developed by the twelve individual units. The working efficiency, or available and usable strength, was the total force developed less the resistance opposed by the cells themselves. The condition is comparable to that of income in the case of an individual or a company; the gross income includes all receipts, from which must be subtracted all costs, if we would determine the net income or actual profit. Or, by another simile, the condition presented by this battery was like that of a mechanical engine, the available efficiency of which is the total energy developed less the effect of friction and all other losses due to imperfect operation.

I was disappointed in the behavior of the battery; its working efficiency was far below what ought to be developed by twelve such units under normal conditions. A casual inspection showed that the cells were not working alike; some of them exhibited intense activity, and in all such the contained liquid was bubbling like boiling water, owing to the escape of liberated gases. The jar was a scene of fuss and fury; yet from such a cell there flowed a current so feeble as to be detectable only with difficulty. The energy developed within those foaming and fuming cells was practically used up in overcoming their own internal resistance, with no surplus power for outside service. I found some cells to be almost inert—with no observable action within, and from such, of course, no current was given out; these cells were practically dead. Certain others were working quietly, with little visible evidence of action aside from the gentle and regular escape of gas bubbles; nevertheless, from the quiet intensity of these, there issued a current potent to transmit messages from continent to continent beneath thousands of miles of ocean turmoil. By diluting the liquid in some jars and intensifying it in others, by replacing a few poorly amalgamated zincs with better ones, and by other modifying adjustments, I succeeded in restraining the wasteful energy of the abnormally active cells, and in arousing to action the dormant ones. The battery was brought into more harmonious operation—just as the restive members of a twelve-horse team might be quieted to steady action, the unwilling ones stimulated, and both brought into unison with their normal and really serviceable fellows.

However, after all such adjustments had been made, the battery was still unsatisfactory. Its operation was weak, irregular, uncertain, and wholly unsuited to the electrolysis required by the work in progress. At length, having become convinced that the fault was a radical one, that some defect was present which no ordinary patching-up process would remedy, I took the battery apart and subjected each cell to an individual examination. One after another passed the test and proved itself to be in measurably perfect condition, until eight had been thus disposed of; the ninth was seriously at fault. This cell was set aside, and the remaining three were tested; all of these were good. Plainly then, the inefficiency of the battery was chargeable to that one unit, number nine; and this, as I remembered, had been among the worst of the abnormally active cells. The eleven good units were connected up; and from the battery thus assembled there issued a current fairly adequate for my needs, and ample to operate an electric receiver or to fire a blast on the opposite side of the globe.

At the first opportunity of convenience I gave closer attention to the rejected unit. There was little difficulty in determining the true cause of the trouble. The cell was in a state of short-circuit; it had short-circuited itself. Through its unnatural intensity of action, as a result of its foaming and fuming, the acid had destroyed the insulation of some parts; and the current that should have been sent forth for service was wholly used up in destructive corrosion within the jar. The cell had violated the law of right action—*it had corrupted itself.* In its defective state it was not only worthless as a working unit, an unproductive member in the community of cells, but was worse than worthless in that it interposed an effective resistance in the operation of the other clean and serviceable units.

Do you wish to know what I did with the unclean cell? I did not destroy it, nor throw it aside as beyond all repair; there was a possibility of its restoration to some measure of usefulness. I searched its innermost parts, and with knife and file and rasp removed the corroded incrustment. I baptized it in a cleansing bath, then set it up again and tried it out in practical employ. Gradually it developed energy until it came to work well—almost as well as the other cells. Yet to this day I watch that unit with special care; I do not trust it as fully as I trusted before it had befouled itself.

I have called this little anecdote of the defective battery a parable; the story, however, is one of actual occurrence. To me there is profound suggestiveness in the incidents related. Even as I wrought in the laboratory, while hands and mind were busy in the work that engaged my close attention, the under-current of thought—the inner consciousness—was making comparison and application.

How like unto those voltaic cells are we! There are men who are loud and demonstrative, even offensive in their abnormal activity; like unto madmen in their uncontrol. Yet what do they accomplish in effective labor? Their energy is wholly consumed in overcoming the internal resistance of their defective selves. There are others who do but sleep and dream; they are slothful, dormant, and, as judged by the standard of utility, dead.

And again, there are men who labor so quietly as scarcely to reveal the fact that they are hard at work; in their utmost intensity there is no evidence of fussy demonstration or wasteful activity; yet such is their devoted earnestness that they influence the thoughts and efforts of the race.

How like a sinner was the unclean cell! Its unfitness was the direct effect of internal disorder, self-corruption, such defection as in man we call sin, which is essentially the violation of law. In association with others who are clean, able, and willing, the sinner is as an obstruction to the current; the efficiency of the whole is lessened if not entirely neutralized, by a single defective unit.

If you would have your personal prayers reach the Divine destination to which they are addressed, see to it that they are transmitted by a current of pure sincerity, free from the resistance of unrepented sin. Let those who assemble in the sacred circle of united prayer have a care that each is individually clean, lest the supplication be nullified through the obstruction of an offending member.

For him who will seek with earnest intent, there is yet other and deeper significance in the parable.

The Parable of the Photographic Plate

On many occasions during long years of professional service as a mining geologist I have been called to the witness stand in court, there to testify under the solemn obligation of oath, as to results of my examination of mines and of lands supposed to contain deposits of valuable minerals. A certain investigation of the kind extended through many months and involved the inspection of numerous tracts of land covering parts of three states. The particular question at issue was the true classification of the several areas as coal-bearing lands or otherwise. As is requisite in such work, a record of all important facts as observed was made in the field and this record, commonly known as the "field notes," was guarded with care, as it would form the basis of all inferences and deductions relating to the investigation.

In due course, more than a year after the completion of the field work, the case came to trial and I was sworn as one of the witnesses. Under both direct and cross examination I was closely questioned concerning the geologic structure and surface conditions of each of the specific tracts and parcels of land. I was permitted to consult my field notes, and so to refresh my memory, as the lawyers said; but, as would be more accurately stated, to assist my recollection of what I had observed while on the ground.

Concerning one section on which no positive indication of coal occurrence had been found, I was interrogated at length as to the character of the surface. Was there timber on this particular piece? Had the land any value for grazing purposes? Was the land level or hilly? To my surprise I found myself unable to answer with certainty. The field notes relating to this particular area were apparently incomplete; the record contained no surface description at all; there was no entry as to timber, grass, or water, no mention of hills or flats. Naturally, I was disappointed and somewhat embarrassed, as in all other descriptions my notes had proved satisfactory. Recollection failed to supply the information called for. Try as I would I could not call to mind just what I had observed. Beyond all doubt I had been upon the ground, for the notes described the corner stone of the sectional division, and gave in detail its measurements and the chiseled notches by which it was identified as an official land-mark. When about to acknowledge my utter inablility to give the data rightly expected of me, just as I was on the point of confessing my seemingly inexcusable failure in a very important part of my work, I was relieved by finding in the note-book one brief entry, which, up to that moment, had escaped my notice. It read simply "S. 10; No. 7." This meant to me that I had taken a photograph at the place referred to in the notes; and the plate on which I would find answer to the questions was No. 7 of Series 10. I had taken many scores of pictures in the course of the long field examination; and the plates had been stored away in the dark room, undeveloped. I asked the court's indulgence until the morrow, promising that then I would furnish conclusive answers to the pending questions.

That night I went to my dark room, and picked out plate No. 7 from the dozen included in Series 10. As shown by the memorandum slip, about fourteen months had passed since that plate had been placed in the camera. With eager expectancy I laid it in the tray and poured upon it the developing liquid. Then, in the faint ruby light of the dark room, lines and shadows gradually appeared,—shall I say like magic? No; but like true miracle, which, however, in this day of popular photography, is counted no miracle but only an ordinary common-place occurrence. When the developing and fixing processes were completed, I examined the plate in a strong light; and there I saw the stone that marked the section corner; there were cattle and my own riding horse, contentedly munching the rich grass, which grew in abundance among stately pines and bright-hued aspen trees; in the foreground was a rippling stream fed by springs, the position of which was discernible in the middle distance of a gentle upland slope. From the negative so produced a print was made; this was taken into court and was there accepted as a full and satisfactory reply to all the questions that had been left unanswered.

The record laid away with the undeveloped plates showed that No. 7 had been exposed a fiftieth of a second. Think of this and forget not the miracle herein made manifest. That plate had been prepared in darkness except for the feeble and nonactinic glow of the ruby lamp; in darkness it had been packed with others in a light-proof box; in darkness it had been transferred to the plate-holder; in darkness it had been placed in the camera, behind the magical wonder-working lens. The coverslide had been withdrawn, leaving the sensitive plate, still in darkness, within the camera box. And then the lens shutter had opened and for *one fiftieth of a second* the plate had looked out upon the glorious landscape, after which, the shutter closed; darkness again enveloped it, and in darkness it lay for a year and more.

For what to us is a measure of time inconceivably short, the light of the glorious truth of day had fallen upon the sensitized surface of the plate, and all through the subsequent months of dense darkness it remembered the heavenly vision. No tree, no leaf, no flower, no grass-blade was forgotten. But mark you, only after the plate had been immersed in the chemical mixture to which it was responsive was the picture brought out so that men might see and know the truth to which it so convincingly testified.

Is the incident worth reading, worth thinking

about? Though of but little merit as a story, it may be of some worth because of the lessons it suggests. Who of us has not realized valuable after-effects from some experience, which, perchance, was relatively as brief and transitory as the view of the sun-lighted scene upon which the photographic plate looked out?

The impress of great truths, caught ofttimes by a momentary flash of heavenly light, are held in store within the hidden recesses of the mind, forgotten, perhaps, for years. Then at a moment of crucial test or painful trial, in the time of distress and affliction, the active reagent compounded in the laboratory of memory and sensitized by the elixir of inspiration is applied, and the picture of the past is brought to light, attesting the truth in a way that none may gainsay or deny.

Let those who minister among their fellows, as teachers of God's word, despair not because of the seeming failure of their efforts. You, my brethren, who through sacrifice and earnest endeavor are devoting yourselves to the saving of souls, be of good cheer, and yield not to the tempter's insinuation that your labors are in vain. It may be that today, by some encouraging word or unselfish act, by some inspired utterance, the full significance of which may have been unrealized by yourselves, you have opened the lens behind which lay a receptive, truth-seeking soul; and though the glory of Divine truth has lightened up that darkened mind for an instant only, the effect is not lost nor will it be forgotten.

Leave the developing of the picture to the Master, who will bring out its lights and its shadows, its verdure and flowers, in his own time, and by means that are to him surest and best.

The Parable of the Owl Express

During my college days, I was one of a class of students appointed to fieldwork as a part of our prescribed courses in geology,—the science that deals with the earth in all of its varied aspects and phases, but more particularly with its component rocks, the structural features they present, the changes they have undergone and are undergoing—the science of worlds.

A certain assignment had kept us in the field many days. We had traversed, examined, and charted, miles of lowlands and uplands, valleys and hills, mountain heights and canyon defiles. As the time allotted to the investigation drew near its close, we were overtaken by a violent wind-storm, followed by a heavy snow,—unseasonable and unexpected, but which, nevertheless, increased in intensity so that we were in danger of being snow-bound in the hills. The storm reached its height while we were descending a long and steep mountain-side, several miles from the little railway station, at which we had hoped to take train that night for home. With great effort we reached the station late at night, while the storm was yet raging. We were suffering from the intense cold incident to biting wind and driving snow; and, to add to our discomfiture, we learned that the expected train had been stopped by snow-drifts a few miles from the little station at which we waited.

The station was but an isolated telegraph-post; the stationhouse comprised but one small room, a mile away from the nearest village. The reason for the maintenance of a telegraph-post at this point was found in the dangerous nature of the road in the vicinity, and the convenient establishment of a water-tank to supply the engines. The train for which we so expectantly and hopefully waited, was the Owl Express—a fast night train connecting large cities. Its time-schedule permitted stops at but few and these the most important stations; but, as we knew, it had to stop at this out-of-the-way post, to replenish the water-supply of the locomotive.

Long after midnight the train arrived, in a terrific whirl of wind and snow. I lingered behind my companions, as they hurriedly clambered aboard, for I was attracted by the engineer, who, during the brief stop, while his assistant was attending to the water replenishment, bustled about the engine, oiling some parts, adjusting others, and generally overhauling the panting locomotive. I ventured to speak to him, busy though he was. I asked how he felt on such a night,—wild, weird, and furious, when the powers of destruction seemed to be let loose—abroad and uncontrolled, when the storm was howling and when danger threatened from every side. I thought of the possibility—the probability even —of snow-drifts or slides on the track; of bridges and high trestles, which may have been loosened by the storm; of rock-masses dislodged from the mountain-side; —of these and other possible obstacles. I realized that in the event of accident through obstruction on or disruption of the track, the engineer and the fireman would be the ones most exposed to danger; a violent collision would most likely cost them their lives. All of these thoughts and others I expressed in hasty questioning of the bustling, impatient, engineer.

His answer was a lesson not yet forgotten. In effect he said, though in jerky and disjointed sentences: "Look at the engine head-light. Doesn't that light up the track for a hundred yards or more? Well, all I try to do is to cover that hundred yards of lighted track. That I can see, and for that distance I know the road-bed is open and safe. And," he added, with what, through the swirl and the dim lamp-lighted darkness of the roaring night, I saw was a humorous smile on his lips, and a merry twinkle of his eye, "believe me, I have never been able to drive this old engine of mine, God bless her! so fast as to outstrip that hundred yards of lighted track. The light of the engine is always ahead of me!"

As he climbed to his place in the cab, I hastened to board the first passenger coach; and, as I sank into the cushioned seat, in blissful enjoyment of the warmth and general comfort, offering strong contrast to the wildness of the night without, I thought deeply of the words of the grimy, oil-stained engineer. They were full of faith—the faith that accomplishes great things, the faith that gives courage and determination, the faith that leads to works. What if the engineer had failed; had yielded to fright and fear; had refused to go on because of the threatening dangers? Who knows what work may have been hindered; what great plans may have been nullified; what God-appointed commissions of mercy and relief may have been thwarted, had the engineer weakened and quailed?

For a little distance the storm-swept track was lighted up; for that short space the engineer drove on!

We may not know what lies ahead of us in the future years, nor even in the days or hours immediately beyond. But for a few yards, or possibly only a few feet, the track is clear, our duty is plain, our course is illumined. For that short distance, for the next step, lighted by the inspiration of God, go on!

The Parable of the Minted Coin

It was once my privilege to make a visit of inspection to the United States Mint at Philadelphia. This is the largest and best equipped establishment of its kind in the country; and within its walls a large proportion of our national coinage is minted, the output ranging from the bronze penny and the nickel piece to the silver dollar with its fractions, thence to the eagle, its half and its double in gold.

I was one of a small party individually invited by the Director of the Mint, under whose official guidance we were conducted through the several departments. In the section devoted to the coining of gold there was great activity, due to the fact that a large issue of eagles, or ten dollar gold-pieces, had been ordered by the Treasury Department, of which the Mint is a bureau. As privileged visitors we were allowed to view the processes at close range from first to last.

We observed the preliminary assay of the gold, and the introduction of the small proportion of base metal to insure the hardness and fineness required by law; then followed the casting of the molten metal into ingots, the rolling of these into strips or fillets each of the exact thickness prescribed. From the thick ribbons of gold, disks were cut, of the diameter and thickness required for the finished coin, and known as blanks or planchets. Though in weight and fineness as true as any eagles in circulation, they were at this stage but smooth pieces of metal; they lacked the stamp that would make them legal tender in the country.

The process that followed next was to me the most impressive of all. The yellow blanks were fed into the great "striking machine" that held the dies. One by one they were delivered to the lower die or anvil; then the arm holding the upper die descended with noiseless precision; and lo! what a moment before had been but an unmarked disk of metal, was now a stamped coin, bearing the attest of the nation as to its genuineness. The pressure exerted upon the piece between the dies was such as to make the gold flow like a viscous mass; a rigid collar confined it, however, and produced the milled edge, while the circular border of the die gave the slight elevation of the rim which is necessary to retard the wearing away of the stamped surface.

Notwithstanding the tremendous force behind the descending die, the operation seemed so gentle, so speedy, and so quiet, as to suggest only a passing touch; nevertheless the imprinted piece will never forget the experience of that moment. Only through disfigurement can it belie its authoritative stamp; only through acid corrosion, long continued attrition, or destructive violence, can the impress be obliterated; and by such defacement the piece would fall below the established standard of value, and would cease to pass as a legal medium of exchange. The stamped disks, no longer blank, but to all appearances finished coins, were then weighed on an automatic balance of extreme precision, by which any chance defective piece was thrown out.

As a true coin of the realm the yellow eagle issued from the mint. Wherever it goes it will bear testimony to the official impress it received in that moment of pressure and stress, to the authority it bears as an intrinsic endowment, a commission, an appointment, such as shall be respected throughout the country and even in other lands, for the credit and the official assurance of the nation are behind the stamp on the coin.

Think of what may be done by virtue of the power possessed by that stamped disk of gold. It may bring food to the famishing, clothing to the needy, professional attendance and skilled nursing to the afflicted; it may help to build a cottage, a mansion, palace, castle, or temple; it may go to pay the way on errands of mercy; it may be made a means of relief and blessing to thousands. With such capacity for good, however, there is correllated a corresponding power for evil. That same gold-piece, because of its official stamp, may buy fuel to feed the flames of lust; it may be bartered for the liquor that corrodes body, mind and soul; it may purchase the bomb that destroys the very structure it once assisted to build; it may pass in exchange for the murderer's weapon, and may even hire the murderer; it may prove a veritable curse to its temporary possessor.

Had it never been touched by the die in the mint, had it not received the stamp that insures it currency, it would be just as truly gold, intrinsically worth the full ten dollars for the metal of which it consists; but it would be of no ready service, since every time it changed hands the receiver would have to weigh it and determine its composition. Such necessity would involve consideration, test, calculation, and withal, hesitation and caution, with possible failure to meet the exigencies of the time.

How like that precious gift of God—the assurance and testimony of the gospel of Christ, how like the bestowal of the gift of the Holy Ghost by the authoritative imposition of hands, how like the divine call and ordination to the Holy Priesthood, is the stamp on the coin! The soul so impressed, so chosen, so ordained, shows by word and act as well as by silent influence, the touch of the finger of God, even though the divine contact has been but momentary.

Like unto those who are honorable in purpose and honest in heart, yet who have not yet yielded obedience to the requirements of the saving gospel, are the unstamped blanks, good metal though they be. Their influence is limited, their capacity for service narrowly circumscribed. They await the touch, the impress that shall commission them to testify and minister in the name of the King.

To every sterling piece such as tallies with the law of righteousness, that touch shall come in the present or the hereafter, provided only the piece be ready. But how will the metal receive the imprint? If it be brittle through base alloy, untempered, unannealed and unyielding, it may break under the stress, or even though it hold together it may present but a blurred similitude of the authoritative stamp.

Oh soul! hast thou not yet passed between the dies? Dost thou await the individual impress of divine commission? And is thy lack due to unreadiness? Art thou tempered and annealed to receive the testimony of God's approval?

And thou other soul, bearing the imprint of such testimony, art thou true to the stamp thou bearest? Unlike the inanimate coin, thou hast agency and the ability to choose in what service thou shalt be used. Thou art of divine mintage. Great is thy power. Fail not!

The Parable of the Unwise Bee

Sometimes I find myself under obligations of work requiring quiet and seclusion such as neither my comfortable office nor the cozy study at home insures. My favorite retreat is an upper room in the tower of a large building, well removed from the noise and confusion of the city streets. The room is somewhat difficult of access, and relatively secure against human intrusion. Therein I have spent many peaceful and busy hours with books and pen.

I am not always without visitors, however, especially in summertime; for, when I sit with windows open, flying insects occasionally find entrance and share the place with me. These self-invited guests are not unwelcome. Many a time I have laid down the pen, and, forgetful of my theme, have watched with interest the activities of these winged visitants, with an afterthought that the time so spent had not been wasted, for, is it not true, that even a butterfly, a beetle, or a bee, may be a bearer of lessons to the receptive student?

A wild bee from the neighboring hills once flew into the room; and at intervals during an hour or more I caught the pleasing hum of its flight. The little creature realized that it was a prisoner, yet all its efforts to find the exit through the partly opened casement failed. When ready to close up the room and leave, I threw the window wide, and tried at first to guide and then to drive the bee to liberty and safety, knowing well that if left in the room it would die as other insects there entrapped had perished in the dry atmosphere of the enclosure. The more I tried to drive it out, the more determinedly did it oppose and resist my efforts. Its erstwhile peaceful hum developed into an angry roar; its darting flight became hostile and threatening.

Then it caught me off my guard and stung my hand, —the hand that would have guided it to freedom. At last it alighted on a pendant attached to the ceiling, beyond my reach of help or injury. The sharp pain of its unkind sting aroused in me rather pity than anger. I knew the inevitable penalty of its mistaken opposition and defiance; and I had to leave the creature to its fate. Three days later I returned to the room and found the dried, lifeless body of the bee on the writing table. It had paid for its stubbornness with its life.

To the bee's short-sightedness and selfish misunderstanding I was a foe, a persistent persecutor, a mortal enemy bent on its destruction; while in truth I was its friend, offering it ransom of the life it had put in forfeit through its own error, striving to redeem it, in spite of itself, from the prison-house of death and restore it to the outer air of liberty.

Are we so much wiser than the bee that no analogy

lies between its unwise course and our lives? We are prone to contend, sometimes with vehemence and anger, against the adversity which after all may be the manifestation of superior wisdom and loving care, directed against our temporary comfort for our permanent blessing. In the tribulations and sufferings of mortality there is a divine ministry which only the godless soul can wholly fail to discern. To many the loss of wealth has been a boon, a providential means of leading or driving them from the confines of selfish indulgence to the sunshine and the open, where boundless opportunity waits on effort. Disappointment, sorrow, and affliction may be the expression of an all-wise Father's kindness.

Consider the lesson of the unwise bee!

"Trust in the Lord with all thine heart; and lean not unto thine own understanding. In all thy ways acknowledge him, and he shall direct thy paths." (Proverbs 3:5, 6).

The Parable of the Treasure-Vault

Neither the story nor its application is the invention of the author; only the telling is his.

Among the news items of recent date was the report of a burglary, some incidents of which are unusual in the literature of crime. The safety-vault of a wholesale house dealing in jewelry and gems was the object of attack. From the care and skill with which the two robbers had laid their plans it was evident that they were adepts in their nefarious business.

They contrived to secrete themselves within the building, and were locked in when the heavily-barred doors were closed for the night. They knew that the great vault of steel and masonry was of the best construction and of the kind guaranteed as burglar-proof; they knew also that it contained treasure of enormous value; and they relied for success on their patience, persistency, and craft, which had been developed through many previous though lesser exploits in safe-breaking. Their equipment was complete, comprising drills, saws and other tools, tempered to penetrate even the hardened steel of the massive door, through which alone entrance to the vault could be effected. Armed guards were stationed in the corridors of the establishment and the approaches to the strong-room were diligently watched.

Through the long night the thieves labored, drilling and sawing around the lock, whose complicated mechanism could not be manipulated even by one familiar with the combination, before the hour for which the time-control had been set. They had calculated that by persistent work they would have time during the night to break open the safe and secure such of the valuables as they could carry; then they would trust to luck, daring, or force, to make their escape. They would not hesitate to kill if they were opposed. Though the difficulties of the undertaking were greater than had been expected, the skilled criminals succeeded with tools and explosives in reaching the interior of the lock; then they threw back the bolts, and forced open the ponderous door.

What saw they within? Drawers filled with gems, trays of diamonds, rubies, and pearls, think you? Such and more they had confidently expected to find and to secure; but instead they encountered an inner safe, with a door heavier and more resistant than the first, fitted with a mechanical lock of more intricate construction than that at which they had worked so strenuously. The metal of the second door was of such superior quality as to splinter their finely tempered tools; try as they would they could not so much as scratch it. Their misdirected energy was wasted; frustrated were all their infamous plans.

Like unto one's reputation is the outer door of the treasure-vault; like unto his character is the inner portal. A good name is a strong defense, but though it be assailed and even marred or broken, the soul it guards is safe, provided only the inner character be impregnable.

The Parable of the Grateful Cat

A certain English student of Natural History, as I have heard, once upon a time had the experience described below.

Mr. Romanes, in the course of his customary daily walk, came to a mill-pond. At the edge of the water he saw two boys with a basket. They were obviously engaged in a diverting occupation. As he came up to them Mr. Romanes observed that the youths were well dressed and evidently somewhat refined and cultured. Inquiry elicited the fact that they were upper servants in a family of wealth and social quality. In the basket were three whining kittens; two others were drowning in the pond; and the mother was running about on the bank, rampant in her distress.

To the naturalist's inquiry the boys responded with a straightforward statement, respectfully addressed. They said their mistress had instructed them to drown the kittens, as she wanted no other cat than the old one about the house. The mother cat, as the boys explained, was the lady's particular pet. Mr. Romanes assured the boys that he was a personal friend of their employer, and that he would be responsible for any apparent dereliction in their obedience to the orders of their mistress. He gave the boys a shilling apiece, and took the three living kittens in charge. The two in the pond had already sunk to their doom.

The mother cat evinced more than the measure of intelligence usually attributed to the animal world. She recognized the man as the deliverer of her three children, who but for him would have been drowned. As he carried the kittens she trotted along—sometimes following, sometimes alongside, occasionally rubbing against him with grateful yet mournful purrs. At his home Mr. Romanes provided the kittens with comfortable quarters, and left the mother cat in joyful content. She seemed to have forgotten the death of the two in her joy over the rescue of the three.

Next day, the gentleman was seated in his parlor on the ground floor, in the midst of a notable company. Many people had gathered to do honor to the distinguished naturalist. The cat came in. In her mouth she carried a large, fat mouse, not dead, but still feebly struggling under the pains of torturous capture. She laid her panting and well-nigh expiring prey at the feet of the man who had saved her kittens.

What think you of the offering and of the purpose that prompted the act? A live mouse, fleshy and fat! Within the cat's power of possible estimation and judgment it was a superlative gift. To her limited understanding no rational creature could feel otherwise than pleased over the present of a meaty mouse. Every sensible cat would be ravenously joyful with such an offering. Beings unable to appreciate a mouse for a meal were unknown to the cat.

Are not our offerings to the Lord—our tithes and our other free-will gifts—as thoroughly unnecessary to His needs as was the mouse to the scientist? But remember that the grateful and sacrificing nature of the cat was enlarged, and in a measure sanctified, by her offering.

Thanks be to God that He gauges the offerings and sacrifices of His children by the standard of their physical ability and honest intent rather than by the gradation of His exalted station. Verily He is God with us; and He both understands and accepts our motives and righteous desires. Our need to serve God is incalculably greater than His need for our service.

The Parable of the Broken Flask

When a youth I left my Utah home and journeyed to the far East to attend college. I matriculated at Lehigh University in Pennsylvania, an institution known then and since for the thoroughness of its courses. For years I had worked, and for a shorter period had taught, with inadequate facilities in an improvised and poorly equipped laboratory. At Lehigh I found myself for the first time in a splendid environment, with all needed accessories of apparatus and material at hand.

Every student was required to make a cash deposit sufficient to cover probable costs of breakage and consumption in the laboratory; and he was then free to call for such instruments and reagents as his appointed work required, with the proviso that all he returned in good condition would be credited to his account and such as he failed to return would be duly charged.

I had no money to spare. With close exactitude I had calculated on probable expenses; and I was conscious of a determination to make a good record both as to scholarship and to promptness and honesty in meeting all pecuniary obligations. I was the first "Mormon" boy to go from our Latter-day Saint schools to the colleges of the East; and in some way I felt—humbly, not egotistically—that I had to maintain and if possible to enhance, certainly not to degrade, the reputation of my people.

During the first week of my laboratory experience in college I had the misfortune to break a large Florence flask—a vessel of thin glass such as is used in many chemical operations, and in that day a more costly utensil than at present. By reference to the price list I ascertained that my carelessness—or perhaps I should say my unskilfulness, for I had tried to be careful— would cost me a dollar. And I would have you know that a dollar looked very big to me in those times.

I was disheartened at the accident. Moreover it had caught me in a state of depression, for I was suffering acutely from a combined attack of two specific maladies, the symptoms of which I have since learned to diagnose with certainty in the case of students who have come under my care—homesickness and lovesickness. Disconsolately I gazed at the fragments of the flask, and then went off to indulge for a brief period in self-communion.

In that hour of weakness and sorrow the evil one tempted me sorely. Through my troubled mind surged thoughts of dire possibilities. What if I should break a dollar flask every week, or possibly oftener? My little store of money might be gone before the school year was half finished. Then I would have to give up, with work uncompleted and hopes defeated. Would it not be better to abandon my plan of laboratory training, and follow instead some minor courses in which only pencil, paper, and library books were needed? Or, better still, why not give up college work altogether? Surely, there were many other fields in which opportunity for service could be found.

Returning to the laboratory I looked ruefully at the broken glass still on my table. Just then one of the graduate students came to my side. I had heard the professors refer to him as a man to whom we could apply for help in their absence. Already I had come to admire his ability and technique. In the hearty way of college men he slapped me upon the back and said "Cheer up, old fellow. Don't mind a little mishap like this. I broke many a flask, and more costly apparatus too, before I learned to do things in the right way."

His words inspired encouragement and determination. If he, a graduate, now engaged in research and original investigation, he, the model worker whose ways we were told to emulate, if he, to whom the instructors pointed as their able substitute, broke expensive glassware and yet succeeded, why could not I go on?

I went on, and in time felt fairly secure in manipulating the most fragile apparatus with a minimum of breakage.

The custom of flaunting coats of arms and family insignia has happily passed. But, had I to select a device to be emblazoned on shield or door, on carriage panel or book mark, supposedly expressive of some determining circumstance in my life, I should be inclined to choose a broken flask; for the recollection of that grievous breakage in the college laboratory has been a means of heartening and uplift in many a crisis of despondency. So may the story be to those who read.

The Parable of the House Party and the Weather

Once upon a time there was a party at our home, even as there had been parties before and have been since; but this one was out of the ordinary. A small company of girls, chums and guests of our girls, had come to spend a few days together, as girls like to do. When was it? Ah, the years have sped their way with swift wings since then! Every one of that gladsome, winsome, lovely and lovable bevy of girls is now a matron in her own right, lovable as ever, with girls of her own—to say nothing of the boys. Never mind the boys; this part of our story has to do with girls. Boys did not count, except as mustn't-meddle lookers-on, in that little house party far back in the yesteryears.

I was a looker-on too, a privileged one in a limited sense, being let into little secrets and whispered conspiracies—for there were factions in the party, each trying to out-do the others in plotting and scheming for the happiness of all.

Blessed be the faculty of recollection! Cheer and comfort come to me tonight as I write—for the indestructible kineograph of the past is clear and brilliant.

The party was a joyous one and a goodly. Every

waking hour was provided for with program varied and full. Wholesome fun and frolic had their place, as had reading, music and story-telling, with just enough of seriousness to make stimulating contrast. Outdoor activities in the early autumn days, with cozy gatherings before the open fire or attendance at theater or concert in the evenings was the usual order.

On my arrival home once at dusk I was forcibly seized—a not unwilling prisoner—and was dragged into the kitchen to view the preparations for next day's picnic. The display was appetizingly tempting. There was to be an early start, for the proposed hike led up City Creek Canyon, thence on beyond Black Mountain, with Dry Canyon as the homeward stretch.

The cumulate knowledge of the group was all-sufficient. They were sure of the trail, where they had to leave the canyon road; they knew just where the late flowers were to be found, where to get the best view of massive limestone walls and crags, where to look for the weathered-out "stone lilies"—those fossilized crinoids that tell of ocean life millenniums ago—all of this and much more. Oh, the joys of anticipation!

I entered into the gladsome spirit of it all, and when released from custody went to my room. Glancing by habit at the barometer hanging above my desk I noted that a very considerable fall in air pressure had occurred during the day, and, as a later reading showed, this was still in progress. A test with the hygrometer demonstrated that the humidity of the atmosphere was unusually high. These observations led to an examination of weather data in the day's paper.

When the evening dinner was finished, as the girls were about to hasten from the table, I ventured to advise that they change their program for the next day and enjoy themselves at or near home, postponing the canyon trip. Then came the inevitable "Why?"

"Because of bad weather: a heavy storm is coming tomorrow." Disappointment was plainly manifest; this led to amazement, and in turn to dismay. I was pulled to the open door, then pushed outside, and was rather peremptorily told to look at the stars. I looked: they were all there, in their places and shining brightly. Questions were put. How could I stand beneath so glorious a sky and speak of rain and wind for the morrow? The prediction, the warning, the advice were repeated; and, of course, the forecaster was made to know that he was very unpopular, then and there. Verily, that poor prophet was without honor in his own household.

Next morning the barometric reading was lower still. No, the barometer had not fallen; to say that it had would be to follow a loose and inaccurate style of speech, all too common. The instrument still hung above my desk, and hangs there yet; but on that bright morning it showed that the atmospheric pressure had decreased or fallen during the night.

At the breakfast table the weather-prophet found his chair shifted from its usual place; it was set so that the direct sunlight would fall upon his plate, if not in his face. After appreciation of the lovely weather had been impressively voiced, somebody made a remark, casual of course, about there being different kinds of prophets. One smiling miss, who was a student in a Church school and whom I had observed in the act of returning the Bible to its place as I came down to breakfast, said that she remembered something in Deuteronomy, eighteenth chapter as she vaguely recalled, about the test of a true prophet being that his predictions came to pass; but weather-prophets were not specifically mentioned in that chapter, she added. The weather-prophet reiterated his forecast and counsel of the preceding evening, with even greater certainty and earnestness.

"Father," said one of our girls, "if you say we mustn't go today, of course we won't. Do you really mean that we must not?"

"No, indeed," was the reply; "I know we shall have a storm today; and to be overtaken by it in the canyon or on the mountain would be not only disagreeable but dangerous. So I advise you to stay near home. But you may do as you please."

The girls went into executive session; a decision was soon reached—to start at once and go as far as they could while the weather was fair; and that *if* any really threatening signs of rain appeared they would turn back.

We left the house at about the same time, the girls and I, they for the canyon, I for the office, they with lunch-baskets, camera, and other accessories, I with rain-coat on arm and umbrella in hand. And the sun was still shining, though clouds could be seen in the north and west.

By early afternoon the sky was darkened, then blackened. Before long lightning flashed and thunder rolled, while the wind roared in fury. The Storm King was abroad, with a mighty army in full action. The possibility of torrents in the canyons caused me concern. I went home early, with mackintosh and umbrella in good service, and with a half-formed plan of enlisting aid and setting out to find the girls. Anxiety was soon dispelled, however. I arrived just in time to witness the return of the bedraggled brigade.

A quick count showed all present, but in what a state! Have you ever seen a flock of chickens rushing for shelter after having been caught afield in a heavy downpour? Never mind answering; the question may have nothing to do with the story—irrelevant indeed.

A bath, dry clothing and dinner restored the feminine spirits to a condition near normal gaiety. They laughed over their misadventures and had much to tell. However, one of the girls guardedly expressed a thought that brought a serious look to every countenance; commotion followed. Then came the most grievous tragedy of the day:

They blamed the weather-prophet for it all—for the rain and the wind, the lightning and thunder, the soaked sandwiches, the torn dresses, and for the loss of sundry articles dropped in the hurried retreat. Why had he cast so evil a spell over them, with his barometer, his hygrometer, and his magical conjurations? Later, they came to understand—in part, at least.

Thank you, girls as you were, women as you are— thank you, each and all, for the good food of thought with which you have served me. I too find it difficult, sometimes, to understand; but is it not so with all of us?

We are prone to confound foreknowledge with cause; and this weakness of ours, absurdly inconsistent, illogical and childish though it be, is particularly manifest in our appraisement of Divine prophecy and its fulfillment. In mercy the Lord warns and forewarns. He sees the coming storm, knows the forces operating to produce it, and calls aloud through his prophets, advises, counsels, exhorts, aye, even commands—that we prepare for what is about to befall and take shelter while yet there is time.

But we go our several ways, feasting and making merry, consoling conscience with the easy fancy of "time enough" and in idle hope that the tempest will pass us by, or that, when it begins to gather thick and black about us we can turn back and find shelter.

So has it been, so is it likely to be, else history is no indicator of futurity. Man is self-centered and selfish; he follows his bent for pleasure, wealth, power, ignoring the barometer of advancing time, though it signals change and turmoil as surely as did the writing on the wall at Belshazzar's impious feast. When the storm bursts—in war, pestilence, famine, earthquake or destruction in general—he attributes evil to the prophets who spake and to the God who gave them utterance.

Pray be not hasty in denying parallelism between the experience of the girls in our story and that of mankind with respect to the great events of history. It may be thought that prophetic warning, based on forknowledge of approaching calamity, would be unnecessary and void if God, who knows all and is almighty—omniscient and omnipotent—chose to avert the impending disaster. True, the human forecaster, depending upon present observations, can tell of coming events only as they cast their shadows before; but one may say that Deity can so order things that there would be no looming disasters to cast shadows and follow them with dread reality. This fragmental thought may be shaped to mean that God could prevent the coming of the storm if *He would*.

Admittedly so, in a narrow sense; *but would He?* By another conception one may rationally and without irreverence ask: *Could He?* As to the attributes of Deity, enough has been revealed to make us know that God operates through law—Divine law—and it follows that He does not violate law. Therefore, God cannot arbitrarily, capriciously, prevent or set aside the results of obedience or disobedience to law.

To the Children of Israel in the olden days, after they had been brought up from Egypt into the land of promise, Jehovah presented two panoramas, of contrast as strong as that between noon and midnight. One showed blessings surpassing all rational expectation, assurance of rich harvests and thriving flocks, of individual and national prosperity; the other depicted misfortune and loss, captivity and servitude. The realization of the one or the other, of blessing or cursing, was contingent upon their fidelity in righteousness or their high treason in sin.

As it became apparent that Israel had chosen the evil alternative, the Lord brought before them again and again the picture of impending distress. He pleaded with them as a father with a wayward son; He commanded and threatened, but they would not heed. In time came the Assyrian captivity, later the Babylonian, and then subjugation by Rome. In accord with the fateful prophecy voiced by Amos, Israel has been scattered amongst the nations "like as corn is sifted in a sieve."

All this was foreknown to Israel's God—yes, and more, for beyond the dispersion He saw the gathering of His people, now in progress. Did Jehovah, whose prescience embraced the events of centuries and millenniums, bring the curse upon Israel, or did Israel bring it upon themselves?

God reads the future of child and children, of men individually and of men collectively as communities and nations; He knows what each will do under given conditions and sees the end from the beginning. His foreknowledge springs from intelligence and supreme wisdom. He sees the future as a state which in the sequence of events will be, not as one which must be because He has willed that it shall be.

The predicted judgments of the last days, now manifest, are just and, withal, beneficent. They were divinely foretold, and the way of escape or protection was prepared aforetime.

So may we apply our parabolic story of the girls and the weather.

The Parable of the Crystal

Do you know what a crystal is? Many have seen the beautiful cubes that form when salt solidifies from the brine; the lustrous octahedrons into which alum shapes itself as the substance separates from a saturated solution; and we may have seen and admired the rhombohedrons of calcite, and the clear hexagonal prisms of quartz, with their pyramidal terminations, each of three or six faces.

In a lump of rock salt the tendency toward crystallization is just as real as in the salt suspended in water as brine, but the bonds of solidity hinders free movement of the ultimate particles, and so prevents the orderly molecular arrangement that is characteristic of the crystal state. Solution is one of the processes by which the molecules of a solid state are so freed from cohesion as to be able to move without hindrance; and another process of similar effect is fusion, or melting under heat. There are many substances for which no physical solvents are known; that is to say we are unable to dissolve them without first converting them into compounds that are soluable.

Like all operations in Nature, the crystallizing process arouses the wonder and taxes the understanding of the observant student. There is something seemingly supernatural in the shaping of the cubes of salt in a saturated brine. Even the unscientific observer sees that the crystal is a manifestation of order; the molecular arrangement is according to system; the symmetry of the crystal is the result of freedom, the freedom of liberty.

Hence we have to say in simile and metaphor, when our ideas on any given subject have been reduced to order and system, that they are crystallized. The figure is a good one, based as it is on sound analogy. To insure the crystallization of ideas through solution, the solvent chosen must be the right one, however rare or precious; aye, though it be the attar of our sweetest fancies, the distillate from false though most-beloved traditions; and to effect crystallization of thought through fusion the requisite temperature must be attained whatever the sacrifice or cost in fuel—though we have to cast into the furnace our fondest superstitions, precious prejudices, and even our very passions of hatred or love.

When a great truth enters one's soul for the first time, the man erroneously calls it a new truth; it may give rise to mental disturbance and possible disruption because it is plainly opposed to the man's earlier conceptions. He has to break down his stubborn traditions, his selfish predilections; with pestle and mortar he must grind them to powder, that thus triturated they may the more readily be dissolved or fused.

THE PARABLE OF THE CRYSTAL

True faith, genuine hope, trust in God, are solvents of rare efficacy; and prayer is the most potent of all. These will in time bring into solution even the most resisting and rebellious thoughts; or, in the furnace, they will develop such heat of conviction as to reduce to quiescent fusion even the most refractory of false beliefs. In the beaker or the crucible new thoughts shall form, freshly crystallized, lustrous, symmetrical, true.

Our Lord—The Christ

The Man Supreme!

In whom dwelt manhood in completeness and the fulness of the Godhead bodily. Under the Father's empowerment the Creator of the heavens and the earth.

Jehovah, the Eternally Existing One who is from everlasting to everlasting, the I AM of eternity past, of time, and of eternity to come.

When the Father called his Chosen, his Beloved Son, his First-born of spirits, his Only Begotten in the flesh.

The Word who was in the beginning, who was with God, who was God, who was made flesh and dwelt among men.

Foremost of all who have trodden the earth with mortal feet.

The Babe of Bethlehem, the Boy of Nazareth, the Man of Sorrows acquainted with grief.

My Elder Brother and yours.

The Teacher Pre-eminent.

He who was condemned as a malefactor, died as a mortal, rose as a God Triumphant.

Redeemer of the race from death, Savior from the effects of sin, source of life eternal.

The first to come from the tomb as a Resurrected Soul.

The Conqueror of death and hell.

He who shall come in like manner as he went and shall reign personally upon the earth with his Saints.

He who shall deliver to the Father the cleansed and purified earth, with its hosts of the redeemed, saying, "I have overcome and have trodden the winepress alone . . . then shall he be crowned with the crown of his glory, to sit on the throne of his power to reign forever and ever." (D&C 76:107-8.)

He has been repeatedly proclaimed by the Father's voice as the Son Divine, and from boyhood to sacrificial death solemnly avowed his own exalted status as that Son of Man. Prophets and apostles in both olden and modern days, and the "common people" who heard him gladly, have reverently affirmed his divinity. Angels have sung and demons shrieked his name as that of power and Godship.

We acclaim Jesus Christ as the veritable Son of the Eternal Father in both spirit and body. He lived as a Man among men yet was wholly unique in that he combined within himself the attributes of mortality as the heritage from a mortal mother and the powers of Godhood received as a birthright from his immortal Father.

Thus he became capable of death and died, yet had power over death, and so held death in abeyance until he willed to die. This he affirmed while yet he was mortal: "Therefore doth my Father love me, because I lay down my life that I might take it again. No man taketh it from me, but I lay it down of myself. I have power to lay it down, and I have power to take it again." (John 10:17-18.)

He was unique in having been accepted and foreordained to be the Redeemer of mankind, and yet again in the fact of his absolute sinlessness.

He was the God of Abraham, Isaac, and Jacob, the *Jehovah* of the Old Testament and the *Christ* of the New.

No man can return to the Father except through the Son, for the name of Jesus Christ is "the only name which shall be given under heaven, whereby salvation shall come unto the children of men."

He has manifested himself, in person to his prophets in the present dispensation, and has spoken with them as one man speaks with another.

He is known to be in the likeness of the Eternal Father—the express image of the Father's person—for both have been seen and heard in this the dispensation of consummation and fulness.

Through the instrumentality of men commissioned to officiate for him, he has re-established his Church upon the earth for the last time, and has bestowed upon it his name—The Church of Jesus Christ of Latter-day Saints.

He has officered his Church as of old, with apostles, patriarchs, high priests, seventies, elders, bishops, priests, teachers, and deacons.

Again as aforetime he has called and is calling mankind to faith and repentance, then to baptism by water, and to the baptism of the Spirit through the bestowal of the Holy Ghost by the authorized imposition of hands.

He manifests his powers through the graces of the Spirit, as seen in gifts of revelation, prophecy, tongues and their interpretation, by inspired dreams and visions, by healings, and by a diversity of gifts called by man miracles.

Through him *redemption* is assured and *salvation* made possible to every soul. Salvation includes and exceeds redemption. It is the plan conceived in the mind of God the Eternal Father and given to man through Jesus Christ, whereby the degenerating and disastrous results of individual transgression may be atoned for; it is the means by which the loathsome malady of sin may be cured. Redemption, or rescue from death, is of universal assurance, salvation is of individual attainment, made possible in fulness through compliance with the laws and ordinances of the gospel based on the *Atonement* accomplished by him alone.

A Redeemer and Savior is essential to the accomplishment of the Father's work and glory "—to bring to pass the immortality and eternal life of man." (Moses 1:39.)

Sometime, somewhere, the knowledge of the Lord shall come to every soul with saving or convicting effect, then every knee shall bow, and every tongue confess that he is the Christ, the Son of the Living God.

The Life of James E. Talmage

"He lived on the bank of a mighty river, broad and deep, which was always silently rolling on to a vast undiscovered ocean. It had rolled on, ever since the world began. . . ."

Those words are attributed to Charles Dickens, the English novelist of the last century. Mr. Dickens could very well have used them to describe a small English lad (who would have been but seven or eight years old when that great man of letters passed away)—James Edward Talmage—who truly lived on the bank of a mighty river of knowledge all through the days of his mortality.

James E. Talmage was born in the small town of Hungerford, Berkshire, England, September 21, 1862—a third generation Latter-day Saint born there in the mission field. He came with his parents to America, arriving in Salt Lake City in June 1876. The family became established at Provo, and James entered the infant Brigham Young Academy (now the University) at the opening of the academic year.

In England James had been a diocesan prize scholar at the age of twelve. At fourteen he entered Brigham

Young Academy, and he and the never-to-be-forgotten master teacher, Karl G. Maeser, discovered each other. Soon James held the positions of secretary to the faculty and academy librarian. In June 1879 he was graduated from the Normal department, and while still in his seventeenth year began teaching philosophy, chemistry, geology, Latin reading (*Julius Caesar*), phonography (the Isaac Pitman system of shorthand), academic penmanship, and grammar, at a weekly stipend of almost 43 cents each, the magnificent sum of $3.00 a week or $120.00 for the school year. The second year his salary increased, but a professor's remuneration left much to be desired.

Before entering the services of the academy he was offered a responsible and an enticing position with the Provo public schools. He needed the money that had been offered. But, following his usual custom, he discussed the matter with his own father, with Brother Maeser, and sought divine guidance. He went to work for the academy.

His field from the beginning of his public life to the end was education, for the early part as a professional teacher, for the latter as a writer and preacher of the word of God. To the classroom he brought such personality, such lucidity of explanation, such an energizing influence that students made unusual progress under his direction. His ready wit was always an engaging part of him in and out of the classroom.

Great honors came to him over the years from the

intellectual world. The man, largely self-taught, was recognized abroad and at home for his original investigations and understanding.

But it was in the spiritual realm that he exercised the greatest influence and felt the strongest call. He impressed one as possessing a severe mind, (his field was first chemistry, and in later years geology), scientific and unusually interested in facts, and then surprised one with the mellowness of his soul and his extraordinary spiritual gifts. Before an audience his persuasion was based largely on logic and intellectual appeal, though he left no doubt of the strength and fervor of his testimony.

In 1932, the late Elder Bryant S. Hinckley, under Era assignment to write biographical articles on members of the Council of the Twelve, asked Dr. Talmage: "When and where did you receive a testimony of the gospel?"

"That I do not know," he answered; "I believe I was born with it as I belong to the third generation of Talmages in the Church. My paternal grandparents, James Talmage of Ramsbury, Wiltshire, England, and his wife, Mary Joyce of Hampshire, England, were the first, or among the first, to join the Church in that part of England. My father, James Joyce Talmage, and my mother, Susannah Preater (Talmage), became members of the Church before I was born. They were active and devoted members.

"Though I seem to have been born with a testimony yet in my early adolescence I was led to question whether that testimony was really my own or derived from my parents. I set about investigating the claims of the Church and pursued the investigation by prayer, fasting, and research with all the ardor of an investigator on the outside. While such a one investigates with a view of coming into the Church if its claims be verified, I was seeking a way out of the Church if its claims should prove to me to be unsound. After months of such inquiry, I found myself in possession of an assurance beyond all question that I was in solemn fact a member of The Church of Jesus Christ. I was convinced once and for all, and this knowledge is so fully an integral part of my being that without it I would not be myself."

Speaking of the priesthood he said: "Every call I have received to office in the priesthood has come to me because some one was needed to fill a particular place, and was in no sense a matter of advancement or honor to myself as an individual. The greatest joys of my life have come to me through activities in the Church, and these have been the activities of a member rather than an officer. Early in life I realized that I would have to live with myself more than with anybody else, and I have tried to so live that I would be in good company when alone."

He desired more education to pursue his chosen field. Many of his friends were strongly against this; and finally Elder Talmage went to see the President of the Church, President John Taylor. In recalling it, Elder Talmage was to say:

"I have often marveled at the kindness and condescension of President Taylor in spending nearly two hours with me. In the course of our conversation he inquired into my work and plans. He advised me strongly to enter a university in the East and, to my grateful surprise, laid his hands on my head and blessed me for the undertaking. The blessing thus pronounced has been realized in both spirit and letter."

As a special student, in 1882, Elder Talmage entered Lehigh University, Bethlehem, Pennsylvania, and in a single year of residence, passed nearly all the requirements of a four-year course and was later graduated from the institution. He was offered a position as laboratory assistant which carried a salary sufficient to meet his needs for the next year, but he declined this offer and went to Johns Hopkins University, Baltimore, Maryland, where he specialized in chemistry and geology during one intensive academic year.

Then he was called home to resume his work at Brigham Young Academy, serving now as professor of geology and chemistry, with varied activities in other departments. During his residence in Provo he served the community as city councilman, alderman, and justice of the peace.

He came to Salt Lake City as president of the Latter-day Saints College, 1888-93, where he also served in the dual capacity of professor of chemistry. In 1894 he became professor of geology and president of the University of Utah, resigning the presidency in 1897 but continuing for ten years as professor of geology. In 1907 he resigned his professorship to follow mining geology.

He received his bachelor of science degree in 1891, and his doctor of science degree in 1912, both from Lehigh University.

As a professional geologist, respected in his field, he literally traveled the earth. The late Elsie Talmage Brandley, one-time associate editor of the Era, prized a birthday letter she had received from her father. He was in Siberia on geologic business—the date: August 1897.

On December 8, 1911, at the age of forty-nine, he was ordained an apostle by President Joseph F. Smith. As such he followed President Joseph Fielding Smith into the Council of the Twelve.

Still he carried a heavy schedule of civic and other activities. He represented Salt Lake City and the State of Utah at the national conventions called to further popular movements. He would plunge into the work at the convention and would bring the enthusiasm home with him.

He was called to preside over the European Mission of the Church in 1924, following President David O. McKay in that assignment. Here came a man to Europe who was not only a leader of a then not so popular church, but he was also a respected and honored Fellow of the Royal Microscopical Society (London), Royal Scottish Geographical Society (Edinburgh), the

Geological Society (London), the Geological Society of America, the Royal Society of Edinburgh, the American Association for the Advancement of Science, and was an Associate of the Philosophical Society of Great Britain, or Victoria Institute. In professional fields he knew whereof he spoke, and when he spoke for the Church, newspaper columns and other media were opened as never before up to that time.

Home again in 1928, Dr. Talmage was finding the challenge of something then comparatively new—radio. The Church had a Sabbath evening radio hour on KSL then as now, and soon he was finding his element. He liked it, and the radio audience enjoyed him. From the March 1929 Improvement Era:

"The sermons delivered over the radio each Sunday evening at nine o'clock, by Dr. James E. Talmage, of the Council of the Twelve, are attracting wide-spread attention. Naturally it would be impossible even to estimate with any degree of accuracy how many people 'listen in,' but it is safe to say that many thousands do. Favorable comments on this series are received from many different states. Our missionaries in Alaska report that they have been able to receive these messages."

He was as much at home in his writing, in his speaking, in his teaching, as he was in his own laboratory. Among his writings were the volumes: *First Book of Nature, Domestic Science, The Great Salt Lake—Present and Past, Tables for the Blowpipe Determination of Minerals, An Account of the Origin of the Book of Mormon, The Articles of Faith, The Great Apostasy, The House of the Lord, The Story of Mormonism, The Philosophical Basis of Mormonism, The Vitality of Mormonism, Jesus the Christ, Sunday Night Talks by Radio.*

He had met with an accident while serving as president of the European Mission that resulted in a knee injury that bothered him, off and on for the rest of his life. Nevertheless he kept working to bring to fruition the great purposes of the restored Church.

The summer of 1933 found him amidst another series of Sunday evening radio sermons. On Tuesday, July 25, he became ill while working at his desk in the Church Offices and was carried to his home. Wednesday found him improved enough to be working at home on his next radio address. On Thursday, July 27, he passed away, death being due to acute miocarditis, following a throat infection.

At the funeral services the following Sunday President J. Reuben Clark, Jr., of the First Presidency, himself a student of Dr. Talmage at the old LDS College, as well as special assistant and private secretary at the University of Utah, paid this tribute:

"To him God's gospel plan was truth, and all truth. Whatever fell outside that plan was error. He literally found

" 'Tongues in trees, books in running brooks; Sermons in stones and good in everything.'

"This was I think, his glory."

Elder Melvin J. Ballard of the Council of the Twelve said:

"In this ministry he produced many volumes that shall be read until the end of time, because that which he has written is so clear and so impressive that it shall ever be among the cherished treasures of those who love the works of God. Yet these contributions he gave freely to the Church, without any earthly reward. . . ."

Elder Ballard that evening read Dr. Talmage's last message to the radio audience, entitled: "Priesthood—Taken from the Earth."

Such was the man James Edward Talmage: gifted and aggressive, a man of brilliant accomplishments and high attainments—student, scholar, preacher, and writer—a man whose very heart and soul found the love of the gospel and spent his all in its purpose and calling.